D1283723

Americans All biographies are inspiring life stories about people of all races, creeds, and nationalities who have uniquely contributed to the American way of life. Highlights from each person's story develop his contributions in his special field — whether they be in the arts, industry, human rights, education, science and medicine, or sports.

Specific abilities, character, and accomplishments are emphasized. Often despite great odds, these famous people have attained success in their fields through the good use of ability, determination, and hard work. These fast-moving stories of real people will show the way to better understanding of the ingredients necessary for personal success.

Quanah Parker

INDIAN WARRIOR FOR PEACE

by LaVere Anderson

illustrated by Russell Hoover

GARRARD PUBLISHING COMPANY
CHAMPAIGN, ILLINOIS

To
Thomas Calvin Thixton, Jr.,
an Oklahoma boy

Picture credits:

Smithsonian Institution, National Collection of Fine Arts: p. 18 (both)
Smithsonian Institution, Office of Anthropology: p. 2, 34, 75, 80, 87 (both)

Contents

1. Captured by Indians

A long-ago spring sun shone down on Fort Parker in Texas. Behind the tall stockade walls, a nine-year-old girl and her two small brothers were playing. Their names were Cynthia Ann, John, and Silas Parker.

They were too young to know that in this year of 1836 Texas was like a battle-field.

White men and red were trying to drive one another from the land. The white settlers wanted to farm and to build towns. The Indians fought to keep the hunting ground that had always been their home.

The children's mother was inside their cabin caring for their baby sister. Grandma Parker sat in the sunny doorway knitting a stocking. Their father worked in the garden some distance away, and in the field beyond the high log walls, other men of the fort were planting corn.

Everything seemed peaceful, but at the stockade gate the children's Uncle Ben stood looking off into the distance as if something troubled him.

Suddenly Uncle Ben shouted, "Indians are coming!"

Cynthia Ann looked up. Through the open gate she could see many Indian warriors racing their ponies toward the fort. She heard the dreadful war whoop that meant the Indians were on a raid. Then a shower of arrows kicked up dust around her.

"Ben is killed!" someone shouted.

Her mother ran from the cabin carrying the baby. "Children, come!" she cried. She caught up tiny Silas's hand, and they all ran toward the small gate at the back of the fort that led to the woods and the river.

But now there came a thunder of hoofs behind Cynthia Ann. She felt herself jerked up in strong arms and lifted to the back of a pony.

She saw another Indian lean low from his pony and swoop up John.

"Cynthia Ann! John!" her mother screamed.

Then the Indians rode from the fort as swiftly as they had come.

The frightened little girl did not know what to do. But she did hold tight to the pony's mane. If she fell to the ground she would be trampled by the horses behind her.

They rode all afternoon. When evening came, they stopped to rest. Cynthia Ann saw that there were a great many Comanche and Kiowa warriors, far more than she could count. She found that they had taken five captives—two women and a little boy besides John and herself.

The Indians dumped their captives on the ground and tied their feet so they could not run away. Cynthia Ann was so tired she fell asleep at once. While she slept, the band divided into smaller groups and many rode off taking John and the other captives along. When she awoke she was alone with some Comanche braves.

Three days of hard riding into far western Texas brought Cynthia Ann's band to their camp. It was in a wide grassy valley beside a stream.

There were many lodges or tepees made of buffalo hide. Nearby a large herd of ponies grazed. When the warriors rode into camp, women and children ran out to meet them. All the dogs barked.

A woman with rings of copper wire around her arms took Cynthia Ann's hand and led her to a lodge. She undressed the little girl and rubbed buffalo fat on her bruises. Then she gave her a dress of deerskin.

Cynthia Ann could not understand the Indian woman's language, but her touch was gentle and her voice sounded kind. When she brought Cynthia Ann some buffalo meat, the little girl ate it hungrily.

12

Days passed, then months, and years. The white girl grew to be a young woman in the Comanche camp.

The Comanches named her Naudah. Her yellow hair darkened from sun and wind. Her skin tanned almost as brown as the Indians'. But her blue eyes showed she was not Indian. In time, she married a chief.

One day a white trader came to the camp. Traders could travel among the Comanches without danger, for they brought many things the red men liked. They brought knives and pans and bright pieces of cloth. They traded these for the Indians' buffalo hides and deerskins.

The trader studied Naudah. At last he said:

"You are a white girl. I think you are Cynthia Ann Parker who was stolen by

Comanches many years ago. Wouldn't you like to go home to your people? I can help you."

The young woman shook her head.

"No, I am Naudah. I am not white any more," she said. "I do not want to go away. I have a good husband. He is a chief and a great hunter."

She pointed to a papoose lying on some skins.

"That is my baby. His name is Quanah, because he was born in the spring, when the smell of earth and new green were strong in the air. Someday he will be a great warrior like his father. I would not leave. These are my people now."

As the trader went away he thought: "Quanah! Half white man, half Indian. I wonder what will happen to that baby when he grows up."

2. White Man's Blood

Six-year-old Quanah watched the other boys swimming and splashing in the Llano River. The Indians called it the River of Wild Hogs because long ago a brave had killed a wild hog on the bank. Quanah did not join in the boys' fun.

Instead, he sat in the water scrubbing himself with a handful of rough weeds. He had already scrubbed so hard that his skin felt sore.

"Look at Quanah!" Little Cloud shouted. "He is trying to wash away his white man's smell."

"Quanah! Quanah!" the others cried.
"No use for him to wash when even his
name means bad smell! He is a white
man. That is why he smells bad. All white
men smell bad."

Quanah scowled at them. "I am
Comanche," he shouted. "My father is
Peta Nocona, great war chief of the
Comanches."

"Your mother is of the white man's people," Bear Tail called. "Can you say that is not true?"

Quanah didn't answer. He ducked his whole body beneath the cold water. Perhaps that would wash away the smell.

The Llano River ran through a great level grassland called the Staked Plains in what is now western Texas. Many buffalo grazed on the rich grass. The Indians said there were as many buffalo as there were leaves on the trees or stars in the sky.

Tribes who made their homes on these rolling plains were called Plains Indians. Among them were many bands of Comanches.

The Comanches did not always stay in one place. They followed the buffalo herds north across the plains in summer,

These paintings show Comanches hunting buffalo (above) and then preparing meat and hides in their village.

south in winter. Buffalo meat was their chief food. They made the shaggy black hides into bed robes, lodges, and clothing. They made the horns into cups and spoons, and the bones into tools. The sinew was made into bowstrings and thread. Even the hoofs could be boiled into glue. Quanah's people could not live without the great humpbacked creatures.

Now Quanah climbed from the river and put on his breech clout and moccasins. Then he went to the circle of lodges.

His mother was cooking. She put a slice of meat on a long green stick and hung it over the fire. His small brother, Pecos, was playing with some pebbles.

"You did not swim long, my son," his mother said.

"I will not swim with those who call me white man," Quanah said scornfully.

Quanah's mother smiled at the boy's angry face.

"You are Comanche," she said. "Pay no attention if the others tease you. It is only boys' talk. They will forget."

Quanah thought about Naudah's words. Then he nodded. "*A-ya.* Yes. I will do as my mother says. I will be such a good Comanche that soon they will not want to tease."

That night Quanah told his father, "I want a big bow and some war arrows. I shall be a great warrior."

"The buffalo will run away when they see such a great warrior coming," his father smiled. "How then will we get any meat?"

But Chief Peta Nocona had a light bow and some arrows made for his little son and gave him a pony for his own.

3. The Buffalo Hunt

Like all Comanche boys, Quanah began to be "grown up" when he was twelve. He worked hard to learn the things a Comanche warrior must know. As time passed everyone forgot that he was half white man.

He learned to shoot an arrow straight to its target and to hurl a lance. He learned to swim and to run fast and long.

He could live off the land, finding nuts and berries to eat, and water holes when he was thirsty.

He could trail an animal or an enemy. He could imitate the hoot of an owl, the gobble of a wild turkey, and the howl of a wolf.

He learned the Indian sign language, and how to send smoke signals. He knew how to stop the bleeding from an arrow or bullet wound.

He could ride a pony and hang from its side or crawl under its belly when it was racing like the wind. He could rope wild horses. He could make sharp bone lances and straight arrows. At last he was old enough to go on a hunt.

The night before the hunt Quanah was too excited to sleep. He lay awake upon his bed of buffalo robes and told himself all the things his father had said he must remember tomorrow.

Go quietly. Do not talk. Make no noise. Buffalo are easily frightened and if they stampede we will lose our winter meat. Do not ride ahead of the others. Wait until the hunt leader gives the signal, then ride fast into the herd and begin shooting. Watch out for any wounded animals. They will charge a rider. Remember that buffalo hunting is no boys' game. It is serious and dangerous business. Hunters who break the rules are not allowed to hunt again for a long time.

"I shall not break the rules," Quanah promised the silvery moon that peeped into the lodge through the open space at the doorway.

Soon it was dawn and time to go. Like all the hunters, Quanah wore only a breech clout and moccasins. Too many clothes would get in the way.

How proudly the boy sat on his pony as he rode out with the men! Nobody spoke, and the hoofs of the unshod horses made scarcely a sound. When the men spotted the herd in the distance, they circled to come up to it against the wind. They wanted no man-smell to alarm the grazing animals.

Quanah's heart was thumping with excitement, but he rode quietly and kept his eyes on the leader. Suddenly the man raised his hand over his head, then dropped it to his side. That was the signal. Quanah kicked his pony into a run. Pell-mell he raced straight into the heart of the great herd. Then all at once he was afraid!

Dust swirled around him, and there was a vast confusion of noise and action. Men shouted. Horses reared. Buffalo plunged right and left in a desperate effort to escape the hunters. Quanah

24

heard the sharp snap of bowstrings and the maddened bellowing of a cow for her calf. He saw dying animals stagger and fall to the ground. For a moment he wanted to run away. Then he shook himself angrily, and his fear passed.

Carefully he fitted an arrow to his bow. Stretching far forward over his pony's head, he aimed at a large buffalo.

How true his arrow sped! It went straight to the chest and through the heart. The big beast dropped to its knees, then to the ground, and lay still.

"Well done, son," said a pleased voice.

Quanah turned to find Chief Peta Nocona riding behind him. He had not known his father was so near, but he was glad that his father had seen the good shot. He did not suspect that the chief had been keeping watch over his son's safety. Peta Nocona remembered his own first hunt and how easy it was for an inexperienced boy to be frightened.

His father cut the tongue from Quanah's first kill. The tongue was the best part of the meat. "Give it to an old man too weak to hunt any more," Peta Nocona said. Quanah knew this was a Comanche custom to teach the young to be kind to old people.

That evening at the feast Quanah did not eat any of the meat from his buffalo. This was a Comanche custom to teach the young not to be greedy.

Happily he watched the others feasting on his kill. Even his new baby sister, Prairie Flower, was sucking on a bone.

"Now I am a hunter," he thought proudly. "Now I shall bring much meat to my mother's cooking fire."

4. Day of Sorrow

Soon the days grew short and the nights cold. It was time for Quanah's people to move to a winter camp.

The Comanches were called a nomadic people because, like all wandering nomads who have no fixed home, they moved so often. It was easy for them to leave one camp and set up another. They had no furniture to carry, only their soft buffalo-hide beds. They had their clothing, small articles such as bowls made from the wood of elm or oak trees, tools of stone or bone, weapons, and pipes.

Sometimes a family had a special treasure such as a small wooden chest brightly painted with earth colors. Earth colors were yellow, red, and brown that came from different colored soils. To make the paint the Indians mixed the colored earth with water and a bit of buffalo sinew. The sinew thickened the paint and made it stick like glue.

When Chief Peta Nocona gave the order to move, everyone became very busy.

The men rounded up the pony herd. The women wrapped their belongings in animal skins and packed them on horses or travois. Travois were crude baskets fastened upon two long poles which were tied to a horse's saddle. The other ends of the poles dragged on the ground. Each buffalo-hide lodge was rolled and packed on a horse, and the stout poles that held up the lodge were tied to the pack saddle and left to drag behind the horse.

In a few hours the band was ready to seek a new camp.

Chief Nocona led them far south to a spot near the beautiful cliffs of the Pease River. The Indians called it Prairie Dog Town River because so many of the furry little animals dug their burrows on the nearby plains.

"*A-ya*. This is a good place," said the Chief. "There is dry grass for our horses and plenty of wood for our campfires."

They unpacked their bundles. They set up their lodges with every door flap facing the east and the rising sun. They dug pits for their fires. They turned their pony herds out to graze. Now they were ready for winter.

But soon there was sadness in the camp. Quanah's people sang the death song because white soldiers were attacking nearby Indian villages and burning the lodges. They were United States cavalry troops sent to punish the Indians for raiding white settlements.

Chief Nocona led his warriors out to avenge their Indian friends. Quanah was still too young to go on a war party.

"Someday I will be old enough," he thought. "I will ride to war beside my father. I will take many scalps and drive the white man from our land."

One day the blue-coated soldiers attacked Quanah's camp. They rode in from two sides, shooting many guns. Women and children ran from the lodges in terror and tried to hide. Warriors grabbed their bows and arrows.

Quanah and his younger brother, Pecos, ran to a nearby creek. They hid in the bushes and listened to the guns. Anger and sorrow filled Quanah's heart.

"Arrows are no good against guns," he whispered bitterly to Pecos.

The battle did not last long. When it ended, Peta Nocona's band had been wiped out. The brave chief was dead.

Naudah was taken captive because the soldiers saw her blue eyes. They knew she was a white woman, and they intended to return her to her people. They took Prairie Flower, too.

The soldiers destroyed every lodge. Then a blizzard came, and the soldiers left.

Quanah and Pecos crept from their hiding place. Icy sleet whipped their faces. The storm was like a white blanket around them. The frightened, freezing boys found that their home and parents were gone. They were alone on the prairie.

"Let us walk," Quanah said. "We will not feel so cold if we keep walking."

At last through the storm Quanah's keen eyes saw some dim moving figures. His sharp ears heard a voice. *"Kee-mah! Kee-mah!"* it called. "Come! Come!"

It was Horseback who called. He was chief of a neighboring band and a ferocious warrior. He was looking for any who had escaped the soldiers.

He took the boys to his camp. A few days later he sent Pecos to another Comanche village where there was a family with no sons. Quanah stayed with Horseback and lived in Horseback's lodge.

Chief Horseback

The half-white boy grew to manhood in Horseback's camp. He rode beside the old chief on many raids against the whites. They burned homes, stole livestock, and took scalps. Quanah was an even more savage warrior than Horseback. He could never forget what the hated white man had done to his family.

"Even Pecos is dead," he thought bitterly. "He grew sick and died in a strange village among strangers. For that, too, I will make the white man pay."

From southern Texas to Kansas no white settlement was safe from Horseback and Quanah.

When Quanah was eighteen years old he organized his own band of Comanches. They were called the Quahadas. Many young braves with their wives and children joined his band. They knew Quanah was a courageous and skillful leader. When they saw he wore an eagle claw hung from a thong around his neck, the braves called him "Quanah, Eagle of the Comanches."

The Comanches were the most hostile and fierce Indians on the plains. Soon the Quahadas were the fiercest of all.

One summer day a scout brought news to Quanah. Quanah called his warriors together.

"The white chiefs want to make peace with the Indians," he said. "They have invited all the southern tribes to a big council meeting. They will sign a peace treaty with us and give us presents. Shall we go?"

"No!" cried some of the braves.

"Yes!" shouted others.

Big Deer spoke up. "I do not trust

their treaties. Many tribes have signed treaty papers. But the papers say one thing and the white man does another. Treaties are papers that talk two ways."

"That is so," agreed Red Leaf. "The white man talks with a crooked tongue. Still it would be wise to go and hear what he is saying now, and I would like to have a present."

They all looked at Quanah. He was the leader. He must decide.

Slowly Quanah began to speak:

"It will be a big pow-wow. There will be many great tribal chiefs there. I have heard their names and deeds. Let those of you who wish, go with me to see these great warriors. Let us take the white man's presents. Let us hear his words and learn if it is peace he wants, or more of our land."

5. To the Pow-Wow

For many days Quanah and his party rode north through the Staked Plains to the meeting place.

It was the end of summer, 1867. Wild grapes were ripe. Leaves of the cotton-wood trees were turning yellow. The young brave looked at his beautiful land with sad eyes. How much longer would it be Indian land, he wondered. More and more white men were moving in.

"They come like ants in a steady stream," he thought. And now he had heard they were building a big iron horse that raced across the plains and never grew tired. It was called a railroad train.

At last the party came to Medicine Lodge Valley where the council was to meet. It was in Kansas on a little branch of the Arkansas River that the Indians called Timber Hill River.

Quanah stared in surprise.

"*Cah-bogn!* Look!" he exclaimed to Red Leaf who rode beside him. "This is an even bigger pow-wow than I thought!"

A thousand Indian lodges were set up for miles along the pleasant stream. To one side the tents of the white soldiers stood in long neat rows. Huge herds of ponies grazed on nearby hills.

Slowly Quanah rode through the encampment. He saw 30 covered wagons filled with white-man goods. He saw big stacks of presents for the Indians. There

were beads and bracelets and useful
things like cooking pots, knives, and
axes. There were blankets, brown sugar,
and tobacco. There were mirrors, paint,
saddles, and bridles.

Best of all, he saw the great chiefs of
his people.

Among the Comanches were Painted
Lips, and the wise old chief, Ten Bears.

In the Apache camp, Crow and Iron
Shirt were pointed out to him. In the
Arapaho camp there were Spotted Wolf
and Little Raven. At the Cheyenne camp
were Black Kettle and Bull Bear. The
famous Satanta was in the Kiowa camp,
and also Kicking Bird.

Five thousand Plains Indians had come
to Medicine Lodge, and many white people. Quanah was excited at seeing such
a large gathering.

"Perhaps there will be peace after all," he told Red Leaf hopefully.

But when the meeting began, he lost hope.

As he listened to the white leaders' words, he began to understand a sad thing. White men did not think they were doing wrong by taking the Indians' land. They thought it was right to plow fields and build houses in the Staked Plains!

"We want to bring civilization to this wilderness," said N. G. Taylor, the Commissioner of Indian Affairs sent by the Great White Father in Washington, D.C.

Commissioner Taylor said the Indians did not need such a vast land. They used it only to hunt. He said the Indians should move to reservations set up for them by the United States Government.

"There you will be fed and cared for," he said. "You won't need to hunt any more."

Other whites made speeches to the red men. They said:

"You must not kill any more white people or steal their cattle and horses. You must not tear up the tracks of the new railroad. You must learn the ways of the reservation and obey the rules. Then everyone can live in peace."

"Peace!" Quanah spat out the word to Red Leaf as though it had a bad taste. "What kind of peace is it if the Indian must live only where the white man puts him and do only what the white man says?"

Many tribal chiefs spoke against the reservation plan. Wrinkled old Ten Bears spoke for the Comanches.

"There has been trouble, but it was not begun by us," he told the white people. "It was you who sent out the first soldier and we who sent the second.

"The blue-dressed soldiers came from out of the night when it was dark and still, and for campfires they lit our lodges.

"You say you want to put us on reservations, to build us houses. I do not want them. I was born on the prairie, where the wind blew free and there was nothing to break the light of the sun. I was born where there were no enclosures and where everything drew a free breath.

"I want to die there, and not within walls."

"*A-ya.* Yes," said the listening Quanah. "We were born free and we must die free."

But the white men paid no attention to Ten Bears. They said the treaty must be signed or else the soldiers would wipe out every Indian village.

Most of the tribal chiefs signed for their people. They were afraid not to sign. But others refused, among them many Comanches.

Quanah said scornfully:

"My band is not going to live on a reservation. Tell the white chiefs that the Quahadas are warriors and will surrender when the blue-coats come and whip us on the Staked Plains."

Then he mounted his pony and rode angrily away. He didn't wait to get his present.

6. Quanah Calls a War Council

It was time for a hunt. The Quahadas needed fresh meat. Their winter supply of dried buffalo meat was nearly gone.

Quanah sent his scouts to find the buffalo herds that returned to the Staked Plains each spring.

When the scouts came back they said:

"There are no buffalo herds. We rode for many sleeps but found only a few small bunches, not enough meat to feed us more than a little while. The great herds are gone."

Quanah's heart grew heavy at their sad words.

Seven springs had passed since the Medicine Lodge Council. The blue-coats had not whipped the Quahadas, but a worse thing had happened.

White hunters with powerful guns had moved onto the plains. They had killed tens of thousands of buffalo. They could sell the thick hides for good prices. They did not want the meat. They left the skinned buffaloes to rot on the prairie, food for only wolves and coyotes.

"This is bad trouble," Quanah said.

He looked around his busy camp and wondered how he could tell his people of the hungry days ahead. Many women were working before their lodges. Some sewed clothing from animal skins while others painted moccasin designs with earth colors or tended cooking fires. Children played nearby. Old people sat in the soft spring sunshine talking of long-ago hunts and battles.

Quanah's face grew sad and sadder still as he watched some braves carefully fitting hawk feathers to new arrows. They were getting ready to go after buffalo. How could he tell them that they would not need those arrows now that the buffalo were gone?

Last of all Quanah looked toward his own lodge. He knew that inside was his wife, Weckeah, and his young children. He had married Weckeah, daughter of Chief Yellow Bear, three years ago. He remembered how, to show his respect for Weckeah, he had given Yellow Bear seventeen ponies. How could he tell Weckeah that soon there would be no food for the children?

Isa-tai was the Quahada medicine man.

He was believed to be very wise and to know the ways of magic. He painted his pony with a yellow "medicine" paint that he said would make bullets bounce off. When he heard the scouts' report he told Quanah, "We must drive the hunters away. The Great Spirit has told me that when they are gone the buffalo will come back."

"Such a battle would take many warriors," Quanah said doubtfully.

"Call a war council of all the tribes. Make a big war plan," Isa-tai advised. "There is no other way to bring back the buffalo."

So again Quanah sent out his scouts. They carried the war message to all the free bands left on the plains.

Soon the chiefs from many camps came to meet with Quanah, for in some camps the people were already beginning to suffer. They heard Isa-tai's words that the Great Spirit promised them victory if they fought the hide hunters.

"There are many hide hunters at a place far from here called Adobe Walls. We must destroy them," said Isa-tai. "Then the buffalo will come back."

"We need the buffalo back," said the chiefs. "The faces of our wives and children grow thin for want of meat."

Quanah filled his war pipe. He offered the first puff of smoke to the sun, the second to the earth, the next to the four winds. Then he sent the pipe around the circle of chiefs.

The chiefs returned to their camps to make ready. The braves sharpened their lances. They feathered arrows. Those who had guns cleaned them well. Isa-tai painted his pony yellow from head to tail.

They danced the war dance. At last it was time to go.

One evening in June 1874, seven hundred warriors met not far from Adobe Walls. It was the largest war party ever gathered on the Staked Plains to fight the whites. They wore war paint and feathers. They carried shields of dried buffalo hide. They had lances and clubs, many arrows, and some guns. Best of all, they thought, they had Isa-tai's magic.

"We will surprise the hunters at dawn and attack them while they sleep," Quanah said. "Isa-tai promises to make strong medicine to help us."

They rode swiftly and silently through the summer night toward Adobe Walls. Their hopes were high. Tomorrow they would win a victory and bring back the buffalo. Life would be good again. *A-ya*. Yes.

52

7. Battle at Adobe Walls

Adobe Walls was a log camp and trading post for buffalo hunters in north Texas. There were several large cabins with strong log walls and roofs made of poles covered with earth. Atop the buildings were protected lookout posts. There was a horse corral, and nearby ran a good-sized creek.

Twenty-eight white hunters were asleep at the post that June night. Two white traders slept in their wagon outside the gate of the corral. They were the only men at Adobe Walls. Their sleep was peaceful, for they did not know that hundreds of war-painted Indians were nearby.

Then a strange thing happened at the post. In the middle of the night a pole holding the roof of one of the buildings broke.

The loud noise awoke the men. They shouted to one another: "Get up! Everybody get up! We must brace the roof or it will fall!" It was almost daylight before they finished the work—much too late to go back to bed.

Young Billy Dixon went outside for his horse which was staked by the creek. Quanah was hiding in the woods beyond the creek. He watched the hunter untie the horse. Back among the trees the warriors waited for the signal to attack.

The first pink streaks of dawn lighted the sky. Birds began to sing. Suddenly Quanah saw the hunter stare into the woods, as though he had seen something move. Then the man reached quickly for his rifle.

Quanah knew they were discovered. The surprise attack was spoiled.

"*Kee-mah!* Come!" he shouted to his warriors.

With angry yells they charged out of the woods, straight at the hunter. He raised his gun and fired a shot to warn his friends. Then he jumped on his horse and raced for the post while arrows zipped around him.

He made it safely, but the braves killed and scalped the two traders sleeping in their wagon and stampeded their horses in the corral. From the cabins the wide-awake hunters sent a shower of bullets into the red ranks.

War whoops and gunfire, dust and smoke, filled the morning air. The first

charge of the Indians carried them right up to the buildings. They beat on the barred doors and windows with club and lance. Some warriors backed their horses violently against the doors and tried to break them in. The reply of the hunters was deadly, and Adobe Walls blazed in the roar of their heavy guns.

Many braves fell in the first charge. The others sent their arrows whizzing through the air only to stick harmlessly in the thick walls.

Again and again the Indians charged. The rising sun gleamed red on their painted faces and tousled feathers. They were beaten back by guns that could drop a 2,000-pound buffalo with one shot from 600 yards away.

The men in the cabins were some of the finest marksmen in the world. Their guns were powerful rifles known as the Sharps "Big 50" or "Buffalo Gun." People said it was "packaged thunder and lightning" that was almost too much gun for any man. Many Indians had only bows and arrows. Some had obsolete "trade" guns that would not shoot far.

Quanah fought bravely. His pony was killed and he found another. He was wounded but kept fighting.

He had known the battle was lost from the moment the hunter fired the warning shot. Quanah had counted on surprising the hunters while they slept. Since the weather was hot, he had thought many of the hunters would be sleeping outdoors. The warriors could surprise them before the hunters were awake to their danger.

Now it was the warriors who had been

surprised. Quanah remembered that long ago he had told Pecos, "Arrows are no good against guns." It was still true.

The battle lasted three days. Many braves were killed, but only one hunter. The hunters stayed safe behind their sturdy walls. Since this was a trading post they had plenty of food and ammunition. There were no portholes in the cabins from which to fire their guns, but through cracks in the logs and from the lookout posts they sprayed death on the red men.

On the third afternoon some Comanches sat talking atop a bluff. Suddenly one toppled from his pony. He had been killed by a shot from the post—nearly a mile away!

"We cannot fight such guns," Quanah said. "They have won the battle."

Sadly the other chiefs agreed. "The white man's gun travels too far," they said. "His gun shoots today and kills tomorrow."

Quanah gave the order for retreat. The weary beaten warriors gathered up their wounded and left. Many blamed Isa-tai for the defeat. His medicine had not worked. Even his painted pony was slain.

"Somebody killed a skunk on the way to battle and spoiled my medicine," Isa-tai declared.

With heavy heart Quanah led his warriors down the long road home. The sorrowing Comanches did not know that Adobe Walls was their last battle. Never again would they smoke the war pipe and ride out to fight for their land and their people.

8. Hunger on the Plains

Quanah stood outside his lodge and looked up at the sky. There was not a cloud anywhere. The sky was like a hot blue roof over the Staked Plains.

He turned to Isa-tai. "Use your medicine to make rain," he said. Isa-tai only looked troubled and walked away.

It had been two moons since the defeat at Adobe Walls. Summer was almost gone. It was the hottest, driest summer Quanah had ever known. Water holes and streams dried up for lack of rain. The grass was like hay. There were deep cracks in the sun-baked earth. The people were suffering.

A party of Comanches and their families rode into the Quahada camp. Quanah saw his old friend High Buffalo of the Nokonis band. He welcomed his friend.

"The words I must speak are bitter as gourds in my mouth," High Buffalo said. "I am taking my people to the reservation. We will surrender."

Quanah was greatly surprised.

"We have no choice," explained High Buffalo. "Word has come from the white men that every warrior must go to his reservation and stay there. He must answer roll call every day. The white men are angry because we fought at Adobe Walls. They are sending their soldiers to find and kill every Indian not on the reservation."

"They won't find me," Quanah said. "We will camp far away. There is no water, and the blue-coats' horses will die on the trail. Their horses are not used to hardships like our ponies. If the soldiers do come near, we will go farther away. They will tire trying to find us."

"They will find you, my friend," High Buffalo said. "There is no place left to hide. And the buffalo are gone." He led his band away.

In the fall the rains came, but now there was too much water. The rains were like floods. Streams overflowed their banks and the ground turned to mud. There were few berries and nuts to eat, and no meat.

The white soldiers were always near. They drove the weary Indians before them like rabbits.

Each time Quanah's people set up a new camp, his scouts brought word that the soldiers were coming again. The Quahadas did not have time to pack all their goods and round up their pony herds. They had to leave much goods and many ponies behind.

In time they lost almost everything— their clothes and lodges and even their cooking pots.

Winter came and it was bitterly cold.
There was no food. A hunter must have
his horse and weapons even to hunt a
deer, and many of these had been left
behind on the long hard marches. The
people were always hungry. Many grew
sick.

Quanah's scouts brought news that
Stone Calf had surrendered his band.
Then the other chiefs surrendered—Lone

Wolf, Red Otter, Swan, and Poor Buffalo, then Red Foot and White Wolf.

Soon the Quahadas were the only free Indians left on the plains.

One day Quanah walked to a sandy hill near his camp. He sat on a rock and drew his robe over his head as a sign of sorrow. He tried to think what to do.

His people were free hunters and warriors. Should he lead them to a reservation where they must dig in the fields? Their children would then grow up in the white man's ways. His own children— what of them? Would they forget the old ways of their ancestors?

But High Buffalo had surrendered and so had Lone Wolf and Stone Calf.

"If I do not surrender, the children and the old and sick will die," Quanah thought. "They need food and care."

He remembered the promises made at Medicine Lodge. Commissioner Taylor had said the Indians would be fed and cared for on the reservation.

"I am a warrior," Quanah told himself. "I would rather die fighting than surrender, but I cannot choose for myself. I must choose for my people."

He pulled the blanket from his head and walked back to camp. His step was firm, for he had chosen.

"*Kee-mah!* Come!" he shouted to the Quahadas. "Everybody get ready. Today we travel a new road."

"What road?" asked a brave.

"The white man's road," Quanah said.

And so the Quahadas started the long journey to the reservation. They were the last band of Comanches to surrender to the white men.

9. On the Reservation

The Comanche reservation lay in western Oklahoma near the Wichita Mountains. It was a beautiful land with wide grassy plains. There was a large log building called the Post. An agent who could speak Comanche gave the Indians supplies and told them where to camp and where to pasture their pony herd. On the way to the reservation Quanah's people had collected all the stray and abandoned ponies they could find. They had a big herd.

Life seemed very strange to the Quahadas for there were many rules to obey. They could not go on hunts or war parties. They were given beef to eat instead of the buffalo meat they liked.

"This *whoa-haw* sticks in our throats," they said of the beef. "We do not like *whoa-haw.*"

Quanah learned sad news about his mother. The agent said she and her baby had died soon after she was returned to her people.

"Why don't you go to Texas and visit her people?" the agent asked. "They are your people too."

"I do not know the road," Quanah said. "I cannot speak English to ask questions."

"I will take care of that." The agent wrote on a piece of paper and handed the paper to Quanah. "Show this if you get lost."

The paper said: "This young man is the son of Cynthia Ann Parker. He is going to visit his mother's people. Please show him the road and help him as you can."

The journey took many days. Finally Quanah came to a good-sized log house covered with bright red trumpet flowers.

A gray-haired man stood at the door. He looked surprised to see a young Indian ride into the yard on a pony. When he read Quanah's paper he held out his hand. "Glad to see you," he said. "Come right in. I'm your Uncle Silas."

He called over his shoulder, "Janey! Here's Cynthia Ann's boy come to see us."

Silas and Janey made Quanah welcome. That night Aunt Janey took him to a bedroom. On the bed were sheets and a pretty flowered quilt.

His aunt said, "Cynthia Ann slept here. Cynthia, her bed." She patted the bed. Quanah knew his mother's white name and understood the gesture. That night he slept between sheets for the first time. They felt different from a buffalo robe.

Everything else was different too. He learned to sit in a chair instead of on the floor. He ate at a table. His spoon was not like the buffalo horn he had always used. Milk tasted queer and so did bread, but he liked molasses.

Many weeks passed. Quanah began to learn to speak English. He watched the white men work in the fields. He saw how they took care of animals, how they sawed wood. He watched the women feed pigs and chickens and churn butter.

"The white man's road is a work road," he thought.

He met many of his relatives. All were kind to him. They told Quanah about his Uncle John who had been captured with Cynthia Ann. John had left the Comanches when he was a grown man. Now he owned a fine ranch in the West.

When Quanah learned that his mother's last name was Parker he added it to his own name.

"Now I am Quanah Parker," he said proudly.

At last it was time to return to the reservation and his family.

"It has been a good visit. I have learned many things," he told his uncle. "I will teach these things to my people."

As he rode away he thought, "It will not be easy to walk the work road. But if my mother could accept Indian ways, I her son can accept white ways."

10. A Hard Road

In the golden sunset of a winter day
Quanah Parker rode back into the
Comanche reservation. He was a different
man from the bitter and hopeless young
Indian who had left last spring. He had
realized in Texas that he now had an
important thing to do.

He must teach his people to accept the
new ways and be friends with the white
man. It was their only chance to be
happy again, he knew. The buffalo were
gone, the plains empty. The red man had
no choice now but to walk the white
man's road.

He began the next morning. As his friends welcomed him home, they told him their troubles.

"While you were away the agent sold many of our ponies and bought us useless sheep and cattle," they complained to Quanah. "The foolish sheep run off and coyotes get them. We killed some of the cattle for meat, but it is not good like buffalo meat. We would rather have our ponies back."

Quanah told them what he had learned about sheep and cattle on his trip. Sheep were foolish, he agreed, but not useless. His uncle kept them tightly penned so they could not stray. Their meat was good to eat, and their hair would make warm blankets. Cattle should not be killed. They should be kept as a start for a herd. In time a few cattle would

Quanah wore his warbonnet when a picture was taken of him in front of his tepee on the Comanche reservation.

grow to be many and they could be sold for money.

Grumbling, the braves left to build pens. It was their first lesson in animal care.

Quanah took wise care of the sheep and cattle that had been saved for him. He traded more of his ponies for more cattle. When spring came Weckeah planted a patch of corn. Quanah practiced his English and made friends with many white men.

One day a brave attacked a white soldier and ran away. It looked like the start of serious trouble between the races.

Quanah found the brave and told him, "This is not good that you have done. Because of you the whole tribe may be punished. Come with me to the agent and take the blame for your own wrongdoing. Then he may not be so hard, and the others will not suffer because of you."

"I do not wish the people to be hurt," said the brave. He went with Quanah. The agent was so surprised to learn the Indians were policing themselves that he gave the brave a light sentence. After that the agent always asked Quanah's advice when there was trouble on the reservation.

Horse thieves began to steal Indian ponies. The Comanches were angry because they could not leave the reservation and go after the thieves. To leave was forbidden. Quanah went to the agent and explained the problem.

"Go find your horses," said the agent.

When the braves heard the news they stood taller. At last they were being treated like men who could fight for their own! With a few other braves Quanah followed the thieves' trail. It was easy for these hunters who, even as children, could follow a deer's faint track. They got back all their own ponies and some of the thieves' horses. Pleased, the agent sent a report to Washington, D.C., about Quanah. Quanah Parker was beginning to make a good name for himself.

When the agent suggested that the Comanches form a police force to guard the plains and herds, the braves refused.

"We are warriors, not police," they said loftily.

Quanah called them to his lodge. "Why do Comanches not want to guard their herds and bring word when someone is sick?" he demanded. "The Cheyennes, since the times of our grandfathers, have had the Dog Soldiers who did such work for the tribe, as well as being leaders in war. Do Comanche braves care less for their people than the Cheyennes?"

It was a new thought to the braves. Many decided to become Indian police.

The agent asked Quanah to find men with wagons to haul supplies from the railroad. Again the braves refused and again Quanah faced them squarely. He said:

"If you were going to a strange place to make war, you would not hold back. You are going to bring back goods that the agent will give out to the whole tribe, instead of war plunder. You will have your own share, too. You will not fight to kill men, but you will have hardships and work to undergo. That takes strong, brave men. Are you afraid?"

Comanches learned to raise cattle on the reservation. This family is butchering one of the herd to add to its food supply.

The shamed Comanches volunteered to haul freight and also to work in the sawmill. Little by little, Quanah was guiding them down the work road.

One day the agent asked for young men to go to the Red River crossing and help Texas cattlemen bring a herd to the reservation. The braves would learn to brand and handle cattle. Each man would be given a few cows for his own.

Quanah would not accept no for an answer. He summoned a number of his warriors and led them to the Red River.

To their surprise, the braves enjoyed the work. It was almost like the old times when they had herded ponies across the plains and at night, under a starry sky, had listened to wolves howling. The cows they earned became the start of the Comanche herds.

On that trip Quanah made a friend. He was Burk Burnett, the big boss of the cattle drive. When the grizzled Texan and the young Comanche chief looked into one another's eyes, a friendship began that was to last a lifetime.

Through Burk Burnett, Quanah came to know the world beyond the prairies.

He visited Burk's ranch, and Burk visited Quanah's lodge on the reservation. Together they went to a stock show at Fort Worth.

It was Quanah's first view of city life. He stood on a busy street corner and marveled at all the people in their fine clothes. Wide-eyed, he stared at the big buildings and the many stores full of pretty things.

"So this is what the white man means by 'civilization!'" he thought. Then he remembered how angry he had been at Medicine Lodge when Commissioner Taylor said the white men wanted to bring civilization to the Staked Plains.

A handsome carriage drawn by two handsome horses rolled down the street. Quanah watched it admiringly. He began to like civilization.

11. "We Are One People"

Swiftly the years sped by. Quanah Parker was so busy he scarcely noticed their passing. The same intelligence and energy that had made him a Quahada chief when he was an eighteen-year-old orphan on the plains now made him a leader in his new life.

He was appointed principal chief of all the Comanches. Under his leadership the Comanches prospered. Then men from the Kiowa and other tribes came to

Quanah's lodge for advice. Soon his word carried power at many council fires.

For a long time the agents on different reservations asked Quanah's help in solving cases of crime. When a Court of Indian Offenses was formed to deal with wrongs done by Indians, Quanah was named the presiding judge. Everyone knew he could be depended on for fair and right decisions.

To his surprise Quanah turned out to be a shrewd businessman. Out on the Staked Plains he had never even heard the word "business." Yet in the white man's world he began to make money.

He started by building up big herds of horses and cattle. Weckeah's first little corn patch grew into a farm of 1,500 acres on which they grew corn, wheat, and sorghum. Quanah hired many men to work on it and to care for the or-chards he set out. With the money he earned from fields and herds, he made wise investments that in turn made more money for him. In time he was said to be the richest Indian in the United States.

He even owned part of a railroad! It was named for him—"The Quanah, Acme and Pacific Railway." Often the tall, straight Indian rode on the train, and sometimes he patted the engine lovingly.

"My train. My engine," he said.

Then he laughed and remembered the days when he used to fear the white man's iron horse.

Yet Quanah was never greedy for money. Once he was offered $5,000 to take a group of Indians on a show tour of Europe. He refused. "I'm no monkey," he said.

He wanted other Indians to have money too. One day he said:

"Cattlemen are grazing their herds on reservation land. The Great White Father said this land was ours. The ranchers must pay us rent for using our land."

The ranchers agreed that this was fair. They paid the Indians $100,000 a year for the pastures. It was called "grass money" and each family got a share. For many families it was the only cash they had. Quanah was generous with his own money too. He gave much to the poor. At heart he was still the same Indian boy who had given the tongue from his first buffalo to an old man and happily went hungry while others feasted on his kill.

One day Quanah decided he needed a house. The old buffalo-hide lodge was too small for his growing family. He

Quanah and one of
his wives posed on
the verandah of his
fine house, below.

built a big two-story white house on land
at the foot of the Wichita Mountains. It
was a beautiful spot and a favorite camp
of Indians in the old days. Quanah had
great white stars painted on the house's
red roof. Those stars could be seen from
miles away. There were twenty-two finely
furnished rooms, and Quanah's family
needed them all. Weckeah had help with
the work for, as was the custom among
the Comanches, Quanah had taken several
wives and he had many children.

Every child was given a good education. At first many Indians protested at
sending their children to the agency
school. They did not want their children
taught "white man."

Quanah talked to them. "The children
who go to school are not hurt," he said.
"They come back to us and live with us,

but they have learned many useful things that will help them get along better than we do when they are grown. The boys are learning how to take care of cattle and to use wagons and make fences. The girls can sew and do many things that their mothers cannot teach them. They learn to speak English and to read and write. All my children shall go to school."

He set the example. Because they trusted his judgment the others sent their children too. Quanah's older children even went to far-away Carlisle School. Quanah helped build schools and helped direct them.

Of all his people, Quanah Parker best understood the need for teaching the children another kind of life from that led by their parents. By now he had traveled far. He had been to Washington, D.C.

many times on tribal business. He and Burk Burnett had attended many stock shows. Quanah's own eyes had seen that there were too many white people and too few Indians. The white man's way must win.

The thought did not make him unhappy. He knew the white man now and saw the good in white ways. He even forgave the man who had captured his mother. That man, a cavalry officer, sent Quanah a photograph of Cynthia Ann taken in her white-woman clothes. Quanah had a large oil portrait painted from the picture. It was his proudest possession. He asked the agent to write a letter to the officer. "Tell this man that my heart is very glad, and that it is good toward him for sending this picture, although it was he who took her away."

To the nation Quanah came to represent not only the Comanche cause but that of all Indians. Leaders from many tribes visited his big white house to pow-wow—even the dreaded Apache fighter, Geronimo. Important white men came, too, among them Ambassador Lloyd from England.

Burk Burnett was a good friend, but Quanah had many others. He became the friend of five Presidents of the United States. His best friend among them was President Theodore Roosevelt. The smiling "Teddy" and Quanah went on wolf hunts together, and the President liked to visit the house with the stars on top.

Not all white people felt the same friendliness for Indians, however. Often Quanah's face fell into sad lines because of their rudeness and disdain.

One day Quanah went into a store. A number of white people were there and they stared at the tall distinguished Indian. He was dressed in a dark business suit, but he still wore his black hair in two long braids. They stared, too, at Quanah's youngest child. He was Chee, and he was all dressed up to go with his father to buy candy.

A young white woman knelt down before the boy, inspecting him. The friendly little fellow held out his arms to be taken up. The woman jumped to her feet with a look of horror. "I wouldn't touch the dirty little Indian for anything in the world!" she exclaimed.

Quanah reached into his vest pocket and pulled out a snapshot. "President Roosevelt did not feel that way and often held him," he told the woman gently.

Then he showed her the picture. It was
the President holding Chee in his arms.

Quanah wanted no more hard feelings
between the races. His days of hate and
anger were past. Once he had been a
warrior in battle, but now he was a warrior for peace, and his ammunition was
love and kindness and patience.

"The government I once fought so hard, I now work for," Quanah said. "I love America and the white man as well as the Indians." He did not think of himself as either Indian or white. He thought of himself as an American. He longed for American citizenship and in time won it for himself and for all his people.

When the braves grew restless and sullen at reservation life, Quanah talked to them like a father soothing a hurt child. When they grew angry and wanted to make war again, he reminded them sternly, "We made war against the whites and we lost."

He taught the Indian to understand the white man, and the white man to understand the Indian.

"We are one people," he said. "We must walk the peace road together."

12. Quanah the Peacemaker

Quanah lived to be an old man, loved and honored by all. He died at his home on a bright February day in 1911. Many newspapers wrote about him, saying the whole nation mourned him and that the respect in which he was held had helped all Indians.

Two thousand white and red men went to his funeral. Speakers told what a great man he was.

Today all over the American Southwest people remember Quanah Parker and name towns, streets, schools, and parks after him. The United States Congress voted money for a fine monument for his grave. The tall red shaft stands in the heart of the land he loved where fresh winds stir the prairie grass and sometimes a hawk wheels overhead.

The words carved on the monument are:

RESTING HERE UNTIL THE DAY BREAKS AND THE SHADOWS FALL AND DARKNESS DISAPPEARS IS QUANAH PARKER, THE LAST CHIEF OF THE COMANCHES.

When President Richard M. Nixon made his Inaugural Address he said: "The greatest honor history can bestow is the title of peacemaker."

History has bestowed that honor on Quanah, for he was a peacemaker.